THE WORLD OF
EGGS

112 DELICIOUS, SWEET AND SAVOURY
EGGS RECIPES
TO ENJOY WITH FAMILY AND FRIENDS.
SUITABLE FOR BEGINNERS.

BY OLIVER TORRES

Table Of Contents

Table Of Contents

Table Of Contents

Table Of Contents

Poached Eggs in Stewed Tomatoes

Ingredients

1 large sweet onion, chopped
1 medium carrot, chopped
1 celery rib, chopped
1/2 cup chopped green pepper
1 garlic clove, minced
2 tablespoons olive oil
2 (14.5 ounce) cans diced tomatoes, undrained
2 tablespoons honey
1 teaspoon chili powder
1/4 teaspoon salt
1/4 teaspoon pepper
1 bay leaf
8 eggs
1/2 cup shredded Cheddar cheese

Directions

In a large skillet, saute the onion, carrot, celery, green pepper and garlic in oil until tender. Stir in the tomatoes, honey, chili powder, salt, pepper and bay leaf. Simmer, uncovered, for 15-20 minutes or until thickened. Discard bay leaf.

With a spoon, make eight indentations in the tomato mixture. Break eggs into indentations. Cover and cook over low heat for 10 minutes or until whites are completely set and yolks begin to thicken. Sprinkle with cheese; cover and cook until cheese is melted, about 1 minute.

Scrambled Eggs a la Jan

Ingredients

8 eggs
1 tablespoon water
1 teaspoon garlic powder
2 1/2 tablespoons mayonnaise
1/4 cup dry white wine
salt and pepper to taste
1/4 cup shredded Cheddar cheese

Directions

Break eggs into mixing bowl. Stir in water, garlic powder, mayonnaise, white wine, salt and pepper. Mix well with a wire whisk. Stir in cheddar cheese.

Heat a nonstick pan over medium heat. Pour in egg mixture and cook, stirring occasionally, until well cooked. The eggs should be firm, but not hard. These eggs will have a softer texture than normal scrambled eggs. Serve warm.

Goldenrod Eggs

Ingredients

2 hard-cooked eggs
2 tablespoons butter
2 tablespoons all-purpose flour
1/2 teaspoon salt
1/8 teaspoon white pepper
1 cup milk
2 slices bread, toasted

Directions

Cut eggs in half; remove yolks and set aside. Chop egg whites; set aside. In a small saucepan, melt butter. Stir in the flour, salt and pepper until smooth. Gradually stir in milk. Bring to a boil; cook and stir for 1-2 minutes or until thickened.

Stir in egg whites; heat through. Pour over toast. Force egg yolks through a sieve to break into small pieces; sprinkle over sauce.

Ingredients

2 cups creamy peanut butter
3/4 cup butter
3 1/2 cups confectioners' sugar
3 cups crispy rice cereal
1 (12 ounce) package semisweet chocolate chips
2 tablespoons shortening

Directions

In a mixing bowl, combine peanut butter and butter. Stir in confectioners' sugar and crisp rice cereal until a dough is formed. Place this mixture in the refrigerator for about an hour to allow it to cool until it is easier to work with. Shape mixture into egg shapes and freeze for 20 minutes.

Melt chocolate chips and shortening in a double boiler over low heat. When melted, dip egg shapes in chocolate. Place on waxed paper and allow to cool.

Lance's Balsamic Pickled Eggs

Ingredients

24 eggs
2 onions, sliced
2 cups balsamic vinegar
4 cups water
4 tablespoons white sugar
20 cloves garlic, mashed into a paste
35 peppercorns
1/2 cup beet juice (see Cook's Note)
6 fresh green and red cayenne chiles, halved lengthwise

Directions

Place the eggs into a large pot cover with water by 1 inch. Cover the saucepan and bring the water to a boil over high heat; remove from the heat and let the eggs stand in the hot water for 15 minutes. Pour out the hot water and cool completely under cold running water; peel and place in a glass jar large enough to hold them.

Combine the onions, balsamic vinegar, water, sugar, garlic, peppercorns, beet juice, and cayenne chiles in a deep saucepan over high heat; bring to a boil and immediately remove from heat. Allow the mixture to cool to room temperature. Pour into the glass jar with the eggs. Seal the jar with the lid. Refrigerate 4 to 5 days before serving.

Savory Baked Eggs

Ingredients

1 medium onion, chopped
1 medium green pepper, chopped
5 tablespoons butter or margarine, divided
6 eggs
1 cup dry bread crumbs
1/4 teaspoon salt
pepper to taste

Directions

In a small saucepan, saute onion and green pepper in 3 tablespoons butter until tender. Transfer to a greased 8-in. square baking dish. Break eggs over the onion mixture. Melt remaining butter; toss with bread crumbs, salt and pepper. Sprinkle over eggs. Place dish in a large baking pan; pour boiling water into larger pan to a depth of 1 in. Bake, uncovered, at 375 degrees F for 12-15 minutes or until the eggs are firm.

Spicy Deviled Eggs

Ingredients

12 eggs
1 1/2 tablespoons Dijon mustard
1 1/2 tablespoons mayonnaise
1/2 teaspoon Worcestershire sauce
1/2 teaspoon hot pepper sauce, or to taste
1 pinch salt and black pepper 1/4 teaspoon ground paprika, for dusting (divided)
1 (6 ounce) can black olives, drained and cut in half horizontally

Directions

Place eggs in a saucepan with a lid, pour in water to cover, bring to a boil, and remove from the heat. Cover and let stand for 10 to 12 minutes. Remove eggs from hot water and let cool. Peel the eggs.

Cut each egg in half lengthwise, remove the yolks, and place the yolks in a bowl with the mustard, mayonnaise, Worcestershire sauce, hot pepper sauce, and salt and pepper. Mash the yolks, and stir the mixture until smooth and thoroughly combined.

Fill each egg half with the deviled yolk mixture, using a spoon, piping bag, or a sturdy plastic bag with a corner cut off. Dust each egg with a pinch of paprika, and place an olive half, round side up, in the center of each. Refrigerate until chilled, 20 to 30 minutes, and serve cold.

Feta Eggs

Ingredients

1 tablespoon butter
1/4 cup chopped onion
4 eggs, beaten
1/4 cup chopped tomatoes
2 tablespoons crumbled feta cheese
salt and pepper to taste

Directions

Melt butter in a skillet over medium heat. Saute onions until translucent. Pour in eggs. Cook, stirring occasionally to scramble. When eggs appear almost done, stir in chopped tomatoes and feta cheese, and season with salt and pepper. Cook until cheese is melted.

Crunchy Chocolate Eggs

Ingredients

1 cup packed brown sugar
1 cup light corn syrup
1 cup peanut butter*
2 cups cornflakes
2 cups crisp rice cereal
1/2 cup finely chopped peanuts
3 3/4 cups semisweet chocolate chips
1 1/2 teaspoons shortening
candy sprinkles

Directions

In a heavy saucepan, combine brown sugar, corn syrup and peanut butter. Cook and stir over medium heat until smooth. Remove from the heat; stir in the cereals and peanuts.

When cool enough to handle, drop by tablespoonfuls onto waxed paper-lined baking sheets. From into egg shapes. Refrigerate until firm. In a microwave, melt chocolate chips and shortening; stir until smooth. Dip eggs in chocolate; allow excess to drip off. Place on waxed paper-lined baking sheets. Decorate with sprinkles. Let stand until set.

Shrimp Deviled Eggs

Ingredients

12 eggs
2 teaspoons butter
1 cup small salad shrimp
1 green onion, chopped
1 pinch garlic powder
1/2 cup mayonnaise, or to taste
1 teaspoon mustard
1/4 cup sweet pickle relish, drained
1 dash hot pepper sauce (optional)
1 tablespoon chopped fresh parsley, or as needed

Directions

Place the eggs into a saucepan in a single layer and fill with water to cover the eggs by 1 inch. Cover the saucepan and bring the water to a boil over high heat. Remove from the heat and let the eggs stand in the hot water for 15 minutes. Drain. Cool the eggs under cold running water. Peel once cold. Halve the eggs lengthwise and scoop the yolks into a bowl. Gently mash the yolks with a fork.

Melt butter in a skillet over medium heat; cook and stir the shrimp, green onion, and garlic powder in the melted butter until, about 4 minutes. Transfer the shrimp to a cutting board and mince. Stir 3/4 cup of the minced shrimp and any remaining liquid from the skillet into the egg yolks; reserve remaining shrimp for garnish. Add the mayonnaise, mustard, pickle relish, and hot sauce; mix well. Scoop the mixture into a resealable plastic bag, seal the bag, and snip a corner off the bag with scissors to make a piping bag.

Gently squeeze about 1 1/2 tablespoon of filling into each egg white half. Garnish each deviled egg with a few pieces of the reserved chopped shrimp and a pinch of the chopped parsley; chill for at least 30 minutes in refrigerator before serving.

Smoked Salmon Deviled Eggs

Ingredients

6 eggs
1 ounce smoked salmon, finely chopped
1 tablespoon mayonnaise
1 1/2 teaspoons fresh lemon juice
1 1/2 teaspoons prepared yellow mustard
1 teaspoon dried dill weed
1/2 teaspoon salt
1 pinch ground black pepper
1/4 teaspoon dried dill weed, for garnish
1 pinch paprika, for garnish

Directions

Place the eggs into a saucepan in a single layer and fill with water to cover the eggs by 1 inch. Cover the saucepan and bring the water to a boil over high heat. Once the water is boiling, remove from the heat and let the eggs stand in the hot water for 15 minutes. Pour out the hot water, then cool the eggs under cold running water in the sink. Peel once cold.

Cut eggs in half lengthwise and scoop out yolks. Mash the yolks with a fork in a small mixing bowl. Mix in the smoked salmon, mayonnaise, lemon juice, yellow mustard, 1 teaspoon dried dill, and the salt and pepper, combining well.

Spoon or pipe the yolk mixture into the egg whites and sprinkle with paprika and a bit of additional dried dill.

Carefully cover with plastic wrap and refrigerate until serving.

Southern Eggs and Biscuits

Ingredients

10 hard-cooked eggs, sliced
1 pound sliced bacon, diced
1/3 cup all-purpose flour
1/4 teaspoon salt
1/8 teaspoon pepper
4 cups milk
2 cups cubed process American cheese
BISCUITS:
1/2 cup shortening
3 cups self-rising flour
1 1/4 cups buttermilk

Directions

Place eggs in the bottom of a greased 13-in. x 9-in. x 2-in. baking dish. In a large skillet, cook bacon until crisp. Drain, discarding all but 1/4 cup drippings. Sprinkle bacon over eggs. Stir flour, salt and pepper into reserved drippings; cook until bubbly. Gradually add milk; cook and stir until thickened and bubbly. Stir in cheese until melted; pour over eggs. For biscuits, cut shortening into flour until mixture resembles coarse crumbs. Stir in buttermilk; knead dough gently six to eight times. Roll out on a lightly floured surface to 1/2-in. thickness. Cut with a 2-1/2-in. biscuit cutter and place on a greased baking sheet. Bake biscuits and eggs at 400 degrees F for 25 minutes or until biscuits are golden brown. Serve eggs over biscuits.

Pizza Eggs

Ingredients

3 slices leftover pizza
2 tablespoons milk
3 eggs
1 teaspoon Italian seasoning
1/8 teaspoon onion powder
salt and black pepper to taste
2 tablespoons vegetable oil

Directions

Scrape the cheese and toppings off the pizza crust, it may help to heat the pizza in the microwave. Discard the crust. Heat the toppings and milk in a small saucepan over medium heat. Stir until the topping and milk combine, it should be a soft clumpy consistency. Remove from the heat.

Heat oil in a skillet over medium heat. Whisk the eggs, Italian seasoning, onion powder, salt, and pepper in a bowl. Pour in eggs and cook without stirring for 1 minute. Add the pizza toppings to the eggs; cook, stirring constantly, until eggs reach the desired consistency.

Garlic Pickled Eggs

Ingredients

12 eggs
1 onion, sliced into rings
1 cup distilled white vinegar
1 cup water
1/4 cup white sugar
10 cloves garlic, peeled

Directions

Place eggs in a medium saucepan and cover with cold water. Bring water to a boil and immediately remove from heat. Cover and let eggs stand in hot water for 10 to 12 minutes. Remove from hot water, cool and peel.

Place the eggs in a 1 quart jar with the onion rings.

In a medium saucepan, bring to a boil the vinegar, water, sugar and garlic. Remove from heat and allow to cool approximately 15 minutes.

Pour the vinegar mixture over the eggs and cover. Refrigerate 1 week before serving.

Debra's Pickled Eggs in Beer

Ingredients

24 small hard-cooked eggs
1 (12 fluid ounce) bottle beer
2 cups vinegar
1 tablespoon pickling spice
1 tablespoon parsley flakes

Directions

Place eggs in a large stock pot and cover with cold water. You may need to cook the eggs in 2 batches if you do not have a pot large enough. Bring to a boil and immediately remove from heat. Cover, and let stand in hot water for 10 to 12 minutes. Cool under cold running water, and peel. Pierce each egg with a knife or fork to assist in the absorption of liquid.

Transfer eggs to a large glass jar or other deep, sealable glass container. Place beer, vinegar, pickling spice, and parsley flakes together in a bowl. Pour over eggs until fully submerged. (Be sure to select a container in which the eggs are completely covered, or add additional pickling liquid, if necessary.) Cover and refrigerate for at least 3 days before using. Can be sealed and stored in the refrigerator for up to 2 weeks in pickling liquid.

Quick and Easy Eggs Benedict

Ingredients

4 slices Canadian bacon
1 teaspoon white vinegar
4 eggs
1 cup butter
3 egg yolks
1 tablespoon heavy cream
1 dash ground cayenne pepper
1/2 teaspoon salt
1 tablespoon lemon juice
4 English muffins, split and toasted

Directions

In a skillet over medium-high heat, fry the Canadian bacon on each side until evenly browned.

Fill a large saucepan with about 3 inches water, and bring to a simmer. Pour in the vinegar. Carefully break the 4 eggs into the water, and cook 2 to 3 minutes, until whites are set but yolks are still soft. Remove eggs with a slotted spoon.

Meanwhile, melt the butter until bubbly in a small pan or in the microwave. Remove from heat before butter browns.

In a blender or large food processor, blend the egg yolks, heavy cream, cayenne pepper, and salt until smooth. Add half of the hot butter in a thin steady stream, slow enough so that it blends in at least as fast as you are pouring it in. Blend in the lemon juice using the same method, then the remaining butter.

Place open English muffins onto serving plates. Top with 1 slice Canadian bacon and 1 poached egg. Drizzle with the cream sauce, and serve at once.

Eggs BenaBabs

Ingredients

1 tablespoon olive oil
2 tablespoons white vinegar
1 quart water
4 artichokes, uncooked and trimmed to the heart
1 recipe Hollandaise Sauce
4 eggs
1 cup black olives, sliced
1/2 cup chopped fresh chives

Directions

Bring olive oil, 1 tablespoon vinegar, and water to boil in a large pot. Place artichoke hearts in the mixture, and boil 30 minutes, or until tender; drain.

Prepare Hollandaise Sauce according to recipe directions.

Fill a large saucepan with 3 inches of water. Bring water to a gentle simmer, and add remaining vinegar. Carefully break eggs into simmering water, and allow to cook for 3 to 5 minutes. Yolks should still be soft in center. Remove eggs from water with a slotted spoon and set on a warm plate.

Place artichoke hearts on a serving platter. Place a poached egg on top of each artichoke heart. Cover with hollandaise sauce. Sprinkle olives on top of sauce. Sprinkle chives around platter.

Cajun-Style Eggs Benedict

Ingredients

2 tablespoons butter
2 tablespoons all-purpose flour
1 cup milk
1/4 cup grated Parmesan cheese
1 dash hot pepper sauce
salt and black pepper to taste

4 large buttermilk biscuits, halved

1/4 cup vegetable oil
1/2 pound andouille sausage,
halved then cut into 2-inch pieces
8 eggs

Directions

Melt the butter in a small saucepan over medium-low heat. Whisk in the flour, and stir until the mixture becomes paste-like and light golden brown, about 3 minutes. Gradually whisk the milk into the flour mixture, and cook over low heat. Cook and stir until the mixture is thick and smooth, about 10 minutes. Stir in the Parmesan cheese and hot sauce; season to taste with salt and pepper. Keep warm over low heat.

Meanwhile, warm the biscuits in a toaster oven and keep warm. Heat the vegetable oil in a large skillet over medium heat. Place the andouille pieces into the skillet cut-side-down. Cook until golden brown, then turn over and cook until browned on the skin side; remove and keep warm. Reduce the heat to medium-low. Crack four of the eggs into the hot pan, and cook until the egg whites have firmed about halfway through, about 1 minute. Gently flip the eggs over, and cook 10 to 20 seconds more until the other side has just firmed on the outside. Repeat with the remaining eggs.

To assemble, place two biscuit halves onto each plate, cut-side-up. Divide the andouille sausage among the biscuits, then top each biscuit with an egg. Finally, spoon some of the sauce over each egg and serve.

Eggs n Bacon Cupcake

Ingredients

2 red potatoes, peeled and grated
2 bulbs shallots, chopped
6 slices bacon, chopped
1/2 cup grated Parmesan cheese
8 eggs, beaten
1 roma (plum) tomato, thinly sliced
1 avocado - peeled, pitted and sliced (optional)

Directions

Preheat the oven to 350 degrees F (175 degrees C). Grease a 12 cup muffin pan with cooking spray.

In a large skillet, fry the bacon pieces over medium heat until browned and crisp, about 8 minutes. Drain off half of the grease. Transfer the bacon and remaining grease to a large bowl. Stir in the shredded potato, shallot and Parmesan cheese. Divide this mixture evenly between the muffin cups. Pour eggs into each cup, filling to the top.

Bake in the preheated oven until the egg is firm, about 12 minutes. Remove from the oven and set the dial to Broil. Place a slice of tomato onto each cupcake and return to the oven. Broil for about 3 minutes, or until toasted. Allow to cool slightly, then arrange the cupcakes on a tray and top each one with a slice avocado, if using.

The Devil's Own Deviled Eggs

Ingredients

12 eggs
1 jalapeno pepper, minced
1 habanero peppers, seeded and minced
1/4 cup mayonnaise
1 teaspoon yellow mustard
1/8 teaspoon paprika

Directions

Place the eggs into a saucepan in a single layer, and fill with water to cover the eggs by at least 1 inch. Bring the water to a boil over high heat. Cover, and remove from the heat; let the eggs stand in the hot water for 15 minutes. Pour out the hot water, then cool the eggs under cold running water in the sink. Peel.

Cut the cooled eggs in half lengthwise. Remove the yolks, and place them into a mixing bowl along with the jalapeno, habanero, mayonnaise, and mustard; mash together until smooth. Transfer the yolk mixture to a pastry bag, and decoratively squeeze into the white halves. Sprinkle with paprika to garnish.

Chutney Eggs

Ingredients

12 eggs
1/4 cup chutney
6 slices bacon
3 tablespoons mayonnaise
1 tablespoon chopped almonds

Directions

Place eggs in a medium saucepan and cover with cold water. Bring water to a boil and immediately remove from heat. Cover and let eggs stand in hot water for 10 to 12 minutes. Remove from hot water, cool and peel. Cut in half lengthwise. Remove and reserve yolks.

Place bacon in a large, deep skillet. Cook over medium high heat until evenly brown; drain and crumble.

In a medium bowl, mash egg yolks and mix with bacon, chutney, mayonnaise and almonds. Fill the egg whites with the mixture.

Balsamic Pickled Eggs

Ingredients

6 eggs
1/2 onion, sliced
1/2 cup balsamic vinegar
1/2 cup water
1 tablespoon white sugar
5 cloves garlic, crushed

Directions

Place eggs in a saucepan and cover with cold water. Bring water to a boil and immediately remove from heat. Cover and let eggs stand in hot water for 10 to 12 minutes. Remove from hot water, cool, and peel.

Place the onion, balsamic, water, sugar, and garlic in a saucepan over high heat. Bring to a boil, then remove from stovetop, and allow to cool to room temperature. Place the eggs in a glass jar, and the vinegar over top. Cover, and refrigerate for 4 to 5 days before serving; the longer the better!

Curried Deviled Eggs

Ingredients

24 eggs
1/2 cup mayonnaise
1/4 cup prepared yellow mustard
2 tablespoons horseradish sauce
2 teaspoons curry powder
1 teaspoon poppy seeds
1 teaspoon chicken bouillon granules
1/2 teaspoon ground coriander
1/2 teaspoon dried minced onion
1/2 teaspoon salt
1/4 teaspoon ground black pepper
1/4 teaspoon ground turmeric

Directions

Place eggs into a large saucepan in a single layer and fill with water to cover the eggs by 1 inch. Cover the saucepan and bring the water to a boil. Remove from heat and let the eggs stand in the hot water for 15 minutes. Drain the hot water; run cold water over the eggs to cool. Peel once cold.

Slice the eggs in half lengthwise; separate the whites and the yolks. Arrange the whites on a large platter; place the egg yolks in a large bowl. Mash the yolks with a fork until smooth; stir the mayonnaise, mustard, horseradish sauce, curry powder, poppy seeds, chicken bouillon granules, coriander, dried minced onion, salt, pepper, and turmeric into the mashed yolks until smooth. Chill the mixture in the refrigerator for 30 minutes.

Spoon the yolk mixture into a heavy plastic bag; snip a corner off the bag to create a 1/2-inch opening. Pipe the yolks into the egg white halves. Serve cold.

Fluffy Scrambled Eggs

Ingredients

8 eggs
1 (5 ounce) can evaporated milk
2 tablespoons butter
salt and pepper to taste

Directions

In a bowl, whisk the eggs and milk until combined. In a skillet, heat butter until hot. Add egg mixture; cook and stir over medium-low heat until eggs are completely set. Season with salt and pepper.

Oven Scrambled Eggs

Ingredients

1/2 cup butter or margarine, melted
24 eggs
2 1/4 teaspoons salt
2 1/2 cups milk

Directions

Preheat the oven to 350 degrees F (175 degrees C).

Pour melted butter into a glass 9x13 inch baking dish. In a large bowl, whisk together eggs and salt until well blended. Gradually whisk in milk. Pour egg mixture into the baking dish.

Bake uncovered for 10 minutes, then stir, and bake an additional 10 to 15 minutes, or until eggs are set. Serve immediately.

Cajun Deviled Eggs

Ingredients

6 eggs
2 tablespoons mayonnaise
1 teaspoon prepared Dijon-style mustard
1/2 teaspoon salt
1/4 teaspoon ground black pepper
1/4 teaspoon ground cayenne pepper

Directions

Place eggs in a medium saucepan and cover with cold water. Bring water to a boil and immediately remove from heat. Cover and let eggs stand in hot water for 10 to 12 minutes. Remove from hot water, cool and peel.

Slice eggs in half lengthwise. Remove yolks and place in a medium bowl. Set aside egg whites. Mashing with a fork, mix mayonnaise, Dijon-style mustard, salt and black pepper with the egg yolks.

Fill the hollowed egg white halves with the yolk mixture. Sprinkle with cayenne pepper, adjusting the amount to taste. Cover and chill in the refrigerator until serving.

Pickled Eggs I

Ingredients

1 (15 ounce) can pickled beets, juice only
1 cup white vinegar
2 1/2 cups water
1/2 cup red wine
1 clove garlic, chopped
1 bay leaf
1 teaspoon pickling spice
1/2 teaspoon salt
12 hard boiled eggs, shells removed
1 onion, chopped

Directions

Drain pickled beets and reserve 1 cup of the juice. Place beet juice, vinegar, water and wine in a large non-reactive glass bowl or jar.

Add garlic, bay leaf, pickling spices, and salt. Mix well. Add eggs and onion rings. Cover tightly, refrigerate for one week before eating.

Emily's Pickled Eggs

Ingredients

12 eggs
1 cup white vinegar
1/2 cup water
2 tablespoons coarse salt
2 tablespoons pickling spice
1 onion, sliced
5 black peppercorns

Directions

Place eggs in a large pot and cover with cold water. Bring water to a boil and immediately remove from heat. Cover and let eggs stand in hot water for 10 to 12 minutes. Remove from hot water, cool and peel. Place the eggs into a 1 quart wide mouth jar.

In a saucepan, combine the vinegar, water, salt, pickling spice, most of the onion (reserve a couple of slices), and black peppercorns. Bring to a rolling boil; pour over the eggs in the jar. Place a couple of slices of onion on top and seal the jars. Cool to room temperature, then refrigerate for 3 days before serving.

Radish Salad With Parsley & Chopped Eggs

Ingredients

2 medium shallots, minced
2 teaspoons Dijon mustard
3 tablespoons rice wine vinegar
Salt and pepper, to taste
1/2 cup extra-virgin olive oil
4 cups thinly sliced radishes
1 cup Italian flat-leaf parsley
(whole leaves, washed, patted dry,
stems discarded), lightly packed
4 large hard-cooked eggs, in small
dice

Directions

Whisk shallots, mustard and vinegar with a generous sprinkling of salt and pepper in a 2-cup measuring cup. Gradually whisk in oil in a slow, steady stream to form a thick dressing. (Can be covered and held at room temperature several hours.)

Place radishes, parsley and chopped eggs in a medium bowl. (Can be covered and refrigerated for several hours.)

When ready, toss with dressing, adjust salt, pepper and vinegar to taste, and serve.

Scotch Eggs

Ingredients

6 eggs
1 pound pork sausage, formed
into 6 patties
4 eggs, beaten
2 cups seasoned bread crumbs
1 quart vegetable oil for frying

Directions

Place eggs in saucepan and cover with water. Bring to boil. Cover, remove from heat, and let eggs sit in hot water for 10 to 12 minutes. Remove from hot water and cool; peel.

In a large deep skillet heat about 1 inch of vegetable oil until hot.

Place whole boiled eggs on top of sausage patty. Roll to form ball around the egg. Dip in beaten egg wash, then seasoned breadcrumbs. Deep fry in hot vegetable oil until meat is fully cooked. Drain and serve hot.

Savory Scrambled Eggs

Ingredients

6 eggs
3 tablespoons mayonnaise
2 tablespoons tomato-based chili sauce

Directions

Heat a large nonstick skillet over medium-low heat. In a medium bowl, whisk the eggs until well blended. When the pan is hot, pour the eggs in. Cook, stirring frequently, until the eggs are scrambled. Nice scrambled eggs should have a soft texture, not hard and leathery.

Remove the eggs from the heat, and stir in the mayonnaise and chili sauce. Serve immediately.

Perfect Scrambled Eggs

Ingredients

1 1/2 tablespoons milk
6 eggs
1/2 cup minced onion 1/2
teaspoon black pepper 1/2
teaspoon salt
1 1/2 teaspoons butter

Directions

Whisk together the eggs, milk, onions, salt, and pepper in a large bowl until it looks slightly fluffy.

Melt the butter in a large pan over medium to high heat; coat the pan evenly with the butter. Stir in eggs and continue stirring until they have just cooked. Serve immediately.

Green Eggs and Ham Breakfast Sandwich

Ingredients

1 (10 ounce) container refrigerated extra large biscuit dough
1/2 pound sliced bacon
3 tablespoons olive oil
1/2 medium onion, chopped
1 jalapeno pepper, seeded and chopped
4 roasted green chile peppers, seeded and chopped
1 teaspoon salt
1 teaspoon pepper
6 eggs
1/2 cup milk
1 cup shredded Monterey Jack cheese

Directions

Prepare biscuits according to the directions on the package. Place bacon in a large, deep skillet. Cook over medium-high heat until evenly brown. Drain, and set aside.

Heat olive oil in a large skillet over medium heat. Add onion, jalapeno, green chile, salt, and pepper. Fry, stirring, until onions are soft. Whisk together the eggs and milk; pour into the skillet. Stir frequently until eggs are scrambled and cooked through.

Split biscuits in half. Place some of the scrambled egg mixture on the bottom half, criss-cross two slices of bacon over the eggs, then top with shredded Monterey Jack cheese. Place the other half of the biscuits on the top, and serve.

Creamy Deviled Eggs

Ingredients

12 eggs
1/3 cup Ranch-style salad dressing
1/2 (8 ounce) package cream cheese, softened
1/2 cup chopped onion
1 dill pickle, finely chopped

Directions

Place eggs in a large saucepan and cover with cold water. Bring water to a boil and immediately remove from heat. Cover and let eggs stand in hot water for 10 to 12 minutes. Remove from hot water, cool and peel.

Slice eggs in half lengthwise and remove yolks. Place yolks in a medium bowl. Mash together with ranch-style salad dressing. Mix in the cream cheese, then the onion and dill pickle.

Fill the hollowed egg whites generously with the egg yolk mixture. Chill in the refrigerator until serving.

Sell Your Soul to the Devil Eggs

Ingredients

12 eggs
4 tablespoons white sugar
1/4 teaspoon salt
1/4 teaspoon onion powder
1/8 teaspoon garlic powder
1/8 teaspoon white pepper
2 tablespoons yellow mustard
1 tablespoon mayonnaise
1 tablespoon creamy salad dressing (such as Miracle Whip®)
1 tablespoon cider vinegar
paprika for garnish (optional)

Directions

Place the eggs in a saucepan in a single layer with enough water to cover by 1 inch. Cover the saucepan and bring the water to a boil over high heat. Once the water is boiling, remove from the heat and let the eggs stand in the hot water for 15 minutes. Pour out the hot water, then cool the eggs under cold running water. Peel once cold.

Dry the eggs thoroughly with paper towels, and slice them in half lengthwise. Remove the yolks, and place in a bowl. Mash the yolks with a fork, and stir in the sugar, salt, onion powder, garlic powder, and white pepper. Add the mustard, mayonnaise, salad dressing, and vinegar, one at a time, stirring to incorporate each ingredient before adding the next.

Mound a heaping teaspoonful of the yolk mixture into the cavity of each egg half, and sprinkle with paprika.

April's Deviled Eggs

Ingredients

4 eggs
1 tablespoon prepared mustard
1 tablespoon mayonnaise
1/2 teaspoon garlic salt
1/2 teaspoon onion powder
1 pinch paprika, for garnish

Directions

Place eggs in a saucepan and cover with cold water. Bring water to a boil and boil eggs for 10 to 15 minutes. Remove eggs from boiling water and place in a medium saucepan of cold water until cool.

Remove the shells and cut the eggs lengthwise to remove the yolks. Place yolks in a medium sized mixing bowl.

Mix in the mustard, mayonnaise, garlic salt and onion powder with the egg yolks. Scoop the mixture into the hollowed out areas of the egg whites. Garnish with paprika. Refrigerate at least one hour before serving.

Zippy Deviled Eggs

Ingredients

12 hard-cooked eggs
1/4 cup mayonnaise
3 tablespoons chili sauce
1 teaspoon prepared mustard
1/4 teaspoon hot pepper sauce
Paprika

Directions

Slice eggs in half lengthwise; remove yolks and set whites aside. In a small bowl, mash yolks. Stir in the mayonnaise, chili sauce, mustard and hot pepper sauce.

Pipe or stuff into egg whites. Sprinkle with paprika. Refrigerate until serving.

Festive Scrambled Eggs

Ingredients

12 eggs
1 1/2 cups milk, divided
1/2 teaspoon salt
1/4 teaspoon pepper
2 tablespoons diced pimientos
2 tablespoons minced fresh parsley or chives
2 tablespoons all-purpose flour
1/4 cup butter or margarine

Directions

In a large bowl, beat eggs and 1 cup milk. Add the salt, pepper, pimientos and parsley. In a small bowl, combine flour and remaining milk until smooth; stir into egg mixture. In a large skillet, melt butter over medium heat. Add egg mixture. Cook and stir over medium heat until the eggs are completely set.

Green Chili Eggs

Ingredients

6 eggs
2 tablespoons milk
1 tablespoon all-purpose flour
2 cups shredded Cheddar cheese
2 (4 ounce) cans chopped green chilies

Directions

Preheat the oven to 375 degrees F (190 degrees C). Grease a 9 inch pie plate.

Whisk the eggs in a large bowl. Stir in the milk and flour, then mix in the green chilies and cheese. Pour into the prepared pie plate.

Bake in the preheated oven until the center is set, about 35 minutes.

Fiesta Scrambled Eggs

Ingredients

1/2 cup chopped onion
1/4 cup chopped sweet red pepper
1 jalapeno pepper, seeded and chopped
8 bacon strips, cooked and crumbled
8 eggs, lightly beaten
1 cup shredded Cheddar cheese, divided
1/2 teaspoon salt
1/8 teaspoon pepper
Salsa

Directions

In a large nonstick skillet coated with nonstick cooking spray, saute the onion and peppers until tender. Sprinkle with bacon. Pour eggs over the top; sprinkle with 1/2 cup cheese, salt and pepper. Cook over medium heat, stirring occasionally, until eggs are completely set. Sprinkle with remaining cheese. Serve with salsa.

Garlic Deviled Eggs

Ingredients

6 hard-cooked eggs
1/3 cup mayonnaise
1/2 teaspoon prepared mustard
2 green onions with tops, chopped
1 garlic clove, minced
1/8 teaspoon salt
Paprika

Directions

Slice eggs in half lengthwise; remove yolks and set whites aside. In a small bowl, mash yolks. Add mayonnaise, mustard, onions, garlic and salt. Fill egg whites; sprinkle with paprika. Refrigerate until serving.

New Orleans Brunch Eggs

Ingredients

1/2 cup finely chopped fresh mushrooms
1/2 cup finely chopped fully cooked ham
1/2 cup finely chopped green onions
2 garlic cloves, minced
2 tablespoons butter or margarine
2 tablespoons all-purpose flour
1/8 teaspoon cayenne pepper
1 1/4 cups beef broth
8 slices grilled ham
8 eggs, poached
4 English muffins, split and toasted

Directions

In a skillet, saute mushrooms, chopped ham, onions and garlic in butter until vegetables are tender. Stir in flour and cayenne pepper. Blend in broth; simmer, stirring occasionally, for 20 minutes. To serve, place a slice of ham and an egg on each muffin half. Spoon sauce over each.

Peppered Shrimp and Eggs

Ingredients

3 bacon strips, diced
3/4 cup chopped green pepper
1/2 cup chopped onion
6 eggs
1/4 cup half-and-half cream
1/2 teaspoon salt
1/4 teaspoon cayenne pepper
1/2 pound cooked large shrimp, peeled, deveined and halved

Directions

In a large skillet, cook bacon over medium heat until crisp. Remove with a slotted spoon to paper towels; drain, reserving 2 tablespoons drippings.

In the drippings, saute green pepper and onion until tender. In a bowl, whisk the eggs, cream, salt and cayenne; add to the vegetable mixture. Add shrimp and bacon. Cook and stir until the eggs are completely set.

Poached Eggs Caprese

Ingredients

1 tablespoon distilled white vinegar
2 teaspoons salt
4 eggs
2 English muffin, split
4 (1 ounce) slices mozzarella cheese
1 tomato, thickly sliced
4 teaspoons pesto
salt to taste

Directions

Fill a large saucepan with 2 to 3 inches of water and bring to a boil over high heat. Reduce the heat to medium-low, pour in the vinegar and 2 teaspoons of salt, and keep the water at a gentle simmer.

While waiting for the water to simmer, place a slice of mozzarella cheese and a thick slice of tomato onto each English muffin half, and toast in a toaster oven until the cheese softens and the English muffin has toasted, about 5 minutes.

Crack an egg into a small bowl. Holding the bowl just above the surface of the water, gently slip the egg into the simmering water. Repeat with the remaining eggs. Poach the eggs until the whites are firm and the yolks have thickened but are not hard, 2 1/2 to 3 minutes. Remove the eggs from the water with a slotted spoon, and dab on a kitchen towel to remove excess water.

To assemble, place a poached egg on top of each English muffin. Spoon a teaspoon of pesto sauce onto each egg and sprinkle with salt to taste.

Stir Fry Tomato and Eggs

Ingredients

2 tablespoons vegetable oil
6 eggs, beaten
1 green onion, chopped
2 large tomatoes, cut into thin
wedges
salt to taste

Directions

Heat the oil in a large skillet over medium heat. When the oil is hot, add the eggs, and green onion; cook and stir until the eggs are almost solid. Add the tomatoes, and cook until eggs are firm. Season with salt, and serve.

Chipotle and Adobo Pickled Eggs

Ingredients

2 cups distilled white vinegar
2 cups water
2 cloves garlic, crushed
1 onion, quartered
1 tablespoon salt
2 tablespoons white sugar
2 canned chipotle chilies
1 tablespoon adobo sauce from canned chipotle peppers
12 hard-cooked eggs, peeled

Directions

In a large pot, combine the vinegar, water, garlic, onion, salt, sugar, chipotle chiles and adobo sauce. Bring to a boil, and cook until the onion is translucent, about 15 minutes.

Place the hard-cooked eggs into clean jars. Strain the boiling brine into the jars to cover the eggs. Cover with lids and refrigerate for at least 3 days before serving. Store in the refrigerator for up to 6 weeks.

Zucchini and Eggs

Ingredients

4 eggs, lightly beaten
2 tablespoons grated Parmesan cheese
2 tablespoons olive oil
1 zucchini, sliced 1/8- to 1/4-inch thick
garlic powder, or to taste
salt and ground black pepper to taste

Directions

Stir the eggs and Parmesan cheese together in a bowl; set aside.

Heat the olive oil in a large skillet over medium-high heat; cook the zucchini in the hot oil until softened and lightly browned, about 7 minutes. Season the zucchini with garlic powder, salt, and pepper. Reduce heat to medium; pour the egg mixture into the skillet. Cook, stirring gently, for about 3 minutes. Remove the skillet from the heat and cover. Keep covered off the heat until the eggs set, about 2 minutes more.

Peanut Butter Easter Eggs

Ingredients

1 (16 ounce) package confectioners' sugar
1 cup creamy peanut butter
1/4 cup butter
1 tablespoon milk
8 (1 ounce) squares semi-sweet chocolate
1 tablespoon shortening

Directions

In a mixing bowl, combine confectioners' sugar, peanut butter, butter and milk (if needed for moisture) until blended. Shape mixture into two 1/2 pound eggs or make a bunch of smaller eggs. Freeze eggs for 1 hour.

While the eggs are freezing, cut semi-sweet chocolate into small pieces and place in top of double boiler with shortening. Melt over medium heat, stirring frequently until smooth. Stick a long-tined fork in top of each peanut butter egg, dip it in melted chocolate to cover then drain on waxed paper. When the eggs are cooled and set, decorate the eggs to suit your fancy.

Poached Eggs in Ginger Syrup

Ingredients

3 cups water
1 cup white sugar
1 (2 inch) piece fresh ginger root, peeled and sliced
4 small eggs

Directions

Combine the water and sugar together in a saucepan and bring to a boil. Reduce heat to medium-low; add the ginger slices and cook until fragrant, about 5 minutes.

Crack the eggs into individual bowls and gently drop them into the syrup. Cook the egg on one side until the white is partially set and opaque, about 3 1/2 minutes; gently turn over to cook the other side until egg white is opaque but not hard, and the yolk is still liquid, about 3 1/2 more minutes or to desired doneness. Spoon the eggs into individual bowls and spoon syrup over each egg. Garnish with the cooked ginger.

Italian-Style Deviled Eggs

Ingredients

12 eggs
1/4 cup chopped prosciutto 1/4
cup grated Parmesan cheese 1/4
cup chopped fresh chives
5 green olives, finely chopped
1/4 cup chopped red bell pepper
1 tablespoon Dijon mustard
1/2 cup sour cream
2 tablespoons mayonnaise
5 dashes hot pepper sauce, such
as Frank's RedHot
1/2 teaspoon garlic powder
1/4 teaspoon ground black
pepper

Directions

Place eggs in a large pot and cover with cold water. Bring water to a boil and immediately remove from heat. Cover and let eggs stand in hot water for 10 to 12 minutes. Remove from hot water, cool and peel.

Slice the eggs in half lengthwise and place the yolks into a bowl and mash with a fork. Set aside some of the Parmesan cheese and chives to use as a garnish. Mix the remaining into the yolks along with the green olives, red bell pepper, Dijon mustard, sour cream, mayonnaise, hot sauce, garlic powder and pepper. Spoon the yolk mixture back into the egg white halves. Garnish with reserved Parmesan cheese and chives.

Bacon-Cheddar Deviled Eggs

Ingredients

12 hard-cooked eggs
1/2 cup mayonnaise
4 bacon strips, cooked and crumbled
2 tablespoons finely shredded Cheddar cheese
1 tablespoon honey mustard*
1/4 teaspoon pepper

Directions

Slice eggs in half lengthwise; remove yolks and set whites aside. In a small bowl, mash yolks. Stir in the mayonnaise, bacon, cheese, mustard and pepper. Stuff into egg whites. Refrigerate until serving.

Kim's Armadillo Eggs

Ingredients

1 (16 ounce) jar whole jalapeno peppers, drained
2 cups shredded Cheddar cheese
1 pound ground pork sausage
2 (10 ounce) cans refrigerated biscuit dough

Directions

Preheat oven to 350 degrees F (175 degrees C).

Slice jalapenos lengthwise to remove seeds. Stuff jalapenos with Cheddar cheese.

Divide ground pork sausage into small balls. Press the sausage balls into thin strips. Place one stuffed jalapeno onto each strip of sausage. Roll the jalapenos in the sausage, pressing it firmly.

Arrange wrapped jalapenos on a medium baking sheet. Bake 40 to 50 minutes in the preheated oven, until sausage is evenly brown. Remove from heat and allow to cool approximately 10 minutes.

Arrange refrigerated biscuit dough on a medium baking sheet. Wrap one sausage and jalapeno roll in each piece of dough.

Bake in the preheated oven 10 to 12 minutes, or until golden brown.

Kimberly's Curried Deviled Eggs

Ingredients

6 eggs
1/4 cup mayonnaise
1 tablespoon stone-ground mustard, or to taste
1 teaspoon curry powder
1/2 teaspoon dried parsley
1 tablespoon sweet pickle relish
1/4 teaspoon ground black pepper
paprika for garnish (optional)

Directions

Place the eggs into a saucepan in a single layer and fill with water to cover the eggs by 1 inch. Cover the saucepan and bring the water to a boil over high heat. Remove from the heat and let the eggs stand in the hot water for 15 minutes. Drain. Cool the eggs under cold running water. Peel once cold. Halve the eggs lengthwise and scoop the yolks into a bowl. Mash the yolks with a fork.

Stir the mayonnaise, mustard, curry powder, parsley, pickle relish, and pepper into the egg yolks until combined; spoon into the egg white halves. Garnish with paprika. Chill before serving.

Red-Chile-Spiked Deviled Eggs

Ingredients

8 large eggs
1/3 cup Hellmann's® or Best Foods® Real Mayonnaise
1 green onion, finely chopped
2 tablespoons finely chopped pickled jalapeno pepper OR dill pickle
2 tablespoons chopped fresh cilantro
2 teaspoons hot pepper sauce
1 1/2 teaspoons ancho chile powder

Directions

Arrange eggs in 2-quart saucepan and cover with cold water. Bring to a boil over high heat. Remove from heat and let stand covered 15 minutes; drain. Cover eggs with cold water and let stand an additional 5 minutes; drain.

Meanwhile, combine remaining ingredients in medium bowl with wire whisk. Season, if desired, with salt and black pepper.

Peel eggs. Slice eggs in half lengthwise and carefully remove yolks. Mash yolks with mayonnaise mixture until smooth.

Spoon mixture into egg whites. Sprinkle, if desired, with additional chili powder and top with cilantro.

Garlic, Basil, and Bacon Deviled Eggs

Ingredients

12 eggs
5 slices bacon
2 large cloves garlic, pressed 1/2
cup finely chopped fresh basil 1/3
cup mayonnaise
1/4 teaspoon crushed red pepper
flakes
salt and pepper to taste
1/4 teaspoon paprika for garnish

Directions

Place the eggs into a saucepan in a single layer and fill with water to cover the eggs by 1 inch. Cover the saucepan and bring the water to a boil over high heat. Remove from the heat and let the eggs stand in the hot water for 15 minutes. Drain. Cool the eggs under cold running water. Peel once cold. Halve the eggs lengthwise and scoop the yolks into a bowl. Mash the yolks with a fork.

Cook the bacon in a large, deep skillet over medium-high heat until evenly browned, about 10 minutes. Drain on a paper towel-lined plate; chop once cool. Add to the mashed egg yolks. Stir the basil, mayonnaise, red pepper flakes, salt, and pepper into the mixture until evenly mixed. Fill the egg white halves with the mixture; sprinkle each stuffed egg with a bit of paprika.

Make-Ahead Scrambled Eggs

Ingredients

2 cups soft bread cubes, crusts removed
1 3/4 cups milk
8 eggs, lightly beaten
3/4 teaspoon salt
1/8 teaspoon pepper
3 tablespoons butter or margarine, divided
2 cups shredded Swiss cheese
1/4 cup dry bread crumbs
6 bacon strips, cooked and crumbled

Directions

Combine bread cubes and milk; let stand 5 minutes. Drain, reserving the excess milk. Place bread in a greased 8-in. square baking dish; set aside. Combine eggs and reserved milk; add salt and pepper. Melt 2 tablespoons butter in a large skillet; add egg mixture and cook just until eggs are set. Spoon over bread cubes. Top with Swiss cheese. Melt remaining butter; add bread crumbs. Sprinkle over cheese. Top with bacon. Cover and chill 8 hours or overnight. Remove from refrigerator 30 minutes before baking. Bake, uncovered, at 350 degrees F for 35 minutes or until heated through. Let stand 5 minutes before cutting.

No-Yolk Deviled Eggs

Ingredients

10 hard-cooked eggs
3/4 cup mashed potatoes
(prepared with skim milk and margarine)
1 tablespoon fat-free mayonnaise
1 teaspoon prepared mustard
2 drops yellow food coloring (optional)
Paprika

Directions

Slice eggs in half lengthwise; remove yolks and refrigerate for another use. Set whites aside. In a small bowl, combine mashed potatoes, mayonnaise, mustard and food coloring if desired; mix well. Stuff or pipe into egg whites. Sprinkle with paprika. Refrigerate until serving.

Chinese Tea Leaf Eggs

Ingredients

8 eggs
1 teaspoon salt

3 cups water
1 tablespoon soy sauce
1 tablespoon black soy sauce
1/4 teaspoon salt
2 tablespoons black tea leaves
2 pods star anise
1 (2 inch) piece cinnamon stick
1 tablespoon tangerine zest

Directions

In a large saucepan, combine eggs and 1 teaspoon salt; cover with cold water. Bring to a boil, reduce heat, and simmer for 20 minutes. Remove from heat, drain, and cool. When cool, tap eggs with the back of a spoon to crack shells (do not remove shells).

In a large saucepan, combine 3 cups water, soy sauce, black soy sauce, salt, tea leaves, star anise, cinnamon stick, and tangerine zest. Bring to a boil, then reduce heat, cover, and simmer for 3 hours. Remove from heat, add eggs, and let steep for at least 8 hours.

Pretzel Eggs

Ingredients

8 egg, beaten
1 tablespoon butter
1 1/2 cups mini pretzels

Directions

In a large skillet, melt butter over medium high heat. Add eggs and pretzels to pan. Cook, stirring occasionally, until eggs are set. Serve hot.

Heart Attack Eggs

Ingredients

6 slices bacon
3 eggs
salt and pepper to taste

Directions

Fry the bacon in a large skillet over medium heat until crisp. Remove from the pan, and set on paper towels to drain. Crack the eggs into the pan with the bacon grease so that they are about 1 inch apart. Season with salt and pepper. When the eggs look firm, flip them over, and cook on the other side to your desired doneness. Transfer to a plate and serve with bacon.

Pen's Deviled Deviled Eggs

Ingredients

12 eggs
1 (4.5 ounce) can deviled ham
1 tablespoon spicy brown mustard
1/4 cup mayonnaise
1 pinch black pepper
24 slices black olives
Paprika for sprinkling

Directions

Place egg in a saucepan and cover with cold water. Bring water to a boil and immediately remove from heat. Cover and let eggs stand in hot water for 10 to 12 minutes. Remove from hot water, cool, and peel.

Cut eggs in half lengthwise, place the yolks into a mixing bowl, and set the whites aside. Mash the yolks with the deviled ham, mustard, mayonnaise, and black pepper. Spoon or pipe filling into egg white halves. Garnish each deviled egg with an olive slice, then sprinkle with paprika.

Scrambled Eggs with Leek and Sauce

Ingredients

2 eggs
1 leek, chopped
1 tablespoon vegetable oil
1 clove garlic, minced
3 tablespoons tomato sauce

Directions

In a small bowl, stir together eggs and chopped leek. Heat the oil in a small skillet over medium heat. Add the egg mixture and cook until set.

Return skillet to heat and add garlic. Saute garlic briefly then add tomato sauce. Pour warm sauce over eggs and serve.

Shirred Eggs

Ingredients

1/4 teaspoon softened butter
2 teaspoons heavy cream
2 eggs
salt and pepper to taste
1 teaspoon minced fresh chives
1 teaspoon grated Parmesan cheese

Directions

Preheat oven to 325 degrees F (165 degrees C).

Rub the inside of a 6 ounce ramekin with butter. Pour cream into the ramekin, then crack the eggs on top of the cream without breaking the yolks. Use a spoon to position the yolks towards the center of the ramekin, then sprinkle with salt, pepper, chives, and Parmesan cheese.

Bake in preheated oven until the whites of the eggs have set and the yolks are still soft, 12 to 15 minutes. Remove from oven, and allow to set for 2 to 3 minutes before serving.

Tasty Eggs for Two

Ingredients

1 cup frozen hash brown potato cubes, thawed
1/4 cup chopped onion
2 tablespoons butter or margarine
1 cup fresh or frozen broccoli florets
1/2 cup julienned fully cooked ham
4 eggs
1 tablespoon milk
1/4 teaspoon lemon-pepper seasoning
1/4 teaspoon dill weed

Directions

In a skillet, cook the potatoes and onion in butter over medium heat until lightly browned, about 10 minutes. Add broccoli; cook until tender. stir in ham. In a bowl, beat eggs, milk, lemon-pepper and dill if desired. Pour over potato mixture; cook for 3-5 minutes or until eggs are completely set, stirring occasionally.

Eggs on the Grill

Ingredients

12 eggs

Directions

Preheat an outdoor grill for medium high heat and lightly oil grate.

Coat all holes of a muffin pan with cooking spray and crack an egg into each hole.

Place on grill and grill over medium high heat for 2 minutes, or to desired doneness.

Avocado Scrambled Eggs

Ingredients

8 eggs
1/2 cup milk
1/2 teaspoon salt
1/4 teaspoon pepper
1 medium ripe avocado, peeled and cubed
2 tablespoons butter or margarine
6 bacon strips, cooked and crumbled

Directions

In a bowl, beat eggs. Add milk, salt and pepper; stir in avocado.

In a skillet over medium heat, melt butter. Add egg mixture; cook and stir gently until the eggs are completely set. Sprinkle with bacon.

Deviled Eggs

Ingredients

6 hard-cooked eggs
2 tablespoons mayonnaise
1 teaspoon sugar
1 teaspoon white vinegar
1 teaspoon prepared mustard
1/2 teaspoon salt
Paprika

Directions

Slice eggs in half lengthwise; remove yolks and set whites aside. In a small bowl, mash yolks with a fork. Add the mayonnaise, sugar, vinegar, mustard and salt; mix well. Stuff or pipe into egg whites. Sprinkle with paprika. Refrigerate until serving.

Creamy Curried Scrambled Eggs

Ingredients

2 teaspoons ghee (clarified butter)
2 shallots, thinly sliced
1 teaspoon curry powder
1 tablespoon water (optional)
4 ounces cream cheese
4 eggs
1 teaspoon Dijon mustard
salt and pepper to taste

Directions

Melt the ghee in a skillet over medium-low heat. Stir in the shallots, and cook until the shallots begin to soften, about 3 minutes. Season with the curry powder, and cook 5 minutes more. Add the tablespoon of water if needed to keep the shallots from burning.

Meanwhile, place the cream cheese into a microwave-safe bowl, and cook in the microwave until the cream cheese is fairly soft, about 30 seconds on High. Whisk in the eggs and Dijon mustard until the cream cheese is mostly mixed in (a few lumps are fine). Stir the egg mixture into the skillet with the shallots, and cook slowly, stirring occasionally, until the eggs have firmed. They will still be softer than normal scrambled eggs because of the cream cheese. Season to taste with salt and pepper just as the eggs are ready to come out of the pan.

Fast and Flavorful Eggs

Ingredients

1/4 cup chopped green pepper
1 tablespoon butter or margarine
6 eggs, lightly beaten
1 (10.75 ounce) can condensed cream of chicken soup, undiluted
3/4 teaspoon salt
1/2 teaspoon pepper
6 bacon strips, cooked and crumbled
1/2 cup milk

Directions

In a skillet, saute green pepper in butter until tender. Combine eggs, 1/2 cup soup, salt and pepper. Add to skillet; cook and stir gently until the eggs are set. Stir in bacon. For sauce, heat milk and remaining soup; stir until smooth. Serve over eggs.

Zucchini and Eggs

Ingredients

2 teaspoons olive oil
1 zucchini, sliced
1 egg, beaten
salt and pepper to taste

Directions

Heat a small skillet over medium heat. Pour in oil and saute zucchini until tender. Spread out zucchini in an even layer, and pour beaten egg evenly over top. Cook until egg is firm. Season with salt and pepper to taste.

Guacamole Deviled Eggs

Ingredients

4 whole eggs in the shell
2 avocados - peeled, pitted, and mashed
1 tablespoon chopped cilantro
1 tablespoon minced green onion
2 teaspoons minced seeded jalapeno pepper
2 teaspoons fresh lime juice
1/2 teaspoon salt, or to taste
1 dash hot pepper sauce (e.g. Tabascoв„ў), or to taste
1 teaspoon Worcestershire sauce, or to taste
1 teaspoon Dijon-style prepared mustard
1 pinch paprika

Directions

Place eggs in a saucepan and cover with cold water. Bring water to a boil and immediately remove from heat. Cover, and let eggs stand in hot water for 10 to 12 minutes. Remove from hot water, cool, and peel. Slice eggs in half, and remove yolks to a mixing bowl.

In the bowl with the yolks, combine the avocado, cilantro, green onion, and jalapeno. Stir in the lime juice, and season with salt, hot sauce, Worcestershire sauce, and mustard. Mix well, and fill empty egg white halves. Chill until serving. Sprinkle with paprika just before serving.

Easy Classic Deviled Eggs

Ingredients

6 hard-cooked eggs
1/3 cup shredded taco-seasoned cheese or Cheddar cheese
1/4 cup mayonnaise
1/4 cup sour cream
3 tablespoons minced green onions

Directions

Cut eggs lengthwise in half. Remove yolks to small bowl. Reserve whites.

Mash yolks with fork. Add cheese, mayonnaise, sour cream and green onions; mix well.

Spoon 1 heaping Tbsp. yolk mixture into each egg white half. Refrigerate, covered, to blend flavors.

Dinosaur Eggs

Ingredients

2 (6 ounce) packages lime gelatin
2 1/2 cups boiling water
1/2 teaspoon ground cinnamon
1 cup cold milk
1 (3.4 ounce) package instant vanilla pudding mix

Directions

In a large bowl, dissolve gelatin in boiling water; let stand at room temperature for 30 minutes. Stir in cinnamon. In a large measuring cup with a spout, beat milk and pudding mix until blended, about 1 minute. Quickly whisk into gelatin until smooth. Pour into a 13-in. x 9-in. x 2-in. pan coated with nonstick cooking spray. Refrigerate for 3 hours or until firm. Cut into ovals or use an egg-shaped cookie cutter.

Smoked Salmon Deviled Eggs and Tomatoes

Ingredients

12 eggs
10 cherry tomatoes, halved and seeded
4 ounces cream cheese, softened
1 (6 ounce) can skinless, boneless salmon, drained and flaked
2 tablespoons mayonnaise
2 tablespoons spicy brown mustard
1 1/2 tablespoons sour cream
1 tablespoon lemon juice
2 tablespoons pickle relish, drained
1/4 teaspoon grated lemon peel, or to taste
1 teaspoon smoked paprika
salt and pepper to taste
smoked paprika for garnish

Directions

Place the eggs into a saucepan in a single layer and fill with water to cover the eggs by 1 inch. Cover the saucepan and bring the water to a boil over high heat. Remove from the heat and let the eggs stand in the hot water for 15 minutes. Drain. Cool the eggs under cold running water. Peel once cold. Halve the eggs lengthwise and scoop the yolks into a bowl. Mash the yolks with a fork.

Place the tomatoes, cut sides down, onto a paper towel to drain.

Mash the cream cheese with a spoon in a bowl until smooth and workable; stir in the egg yolks, salmon, mayonnaise, brown mustard, sour cream, lemon juice, pickle relish, lemon peel, and 1 teaspoon of smoked paprika until well combined. Season with salt and pepper.

Spoon the salmon mixture into the egg halves and cherry tomato halves. Sprinkle with additional smoked paprika for garnish and arrange on a platter. Chill at least 1 hour before serving.

Cheeseburger-Topped Scrambled Eggs

Ingredients

4 fully-cooked turkey breakfast
sausage patties
4 eggs
4 tablespoons milk
Salt and pepper
2 teaspoons butter
2 slices American cheese, halved
Ketchup
Pickles

Directions

Heat sausage according to package directions; keep warm.

Beat eggs, milk, salt and pepper in bowl until blended.

Heat butter in nonstick skillet over medium heat until hot. Pour in egg mixture. As eggs begin to set, gently pull the eggs across the pan with an inverted turner, forming large soft curds.

Continue cooking--pulling, lifting and folding eggs--until thickened and no visible liquid egg remains. Do not stir constantly. Remove from heat.

Place sausage patties on microwave-safe plate. Top evenly with eggs, then with cheese. Microwave on High a few seconds, just to melt cheese. Top with ketchup and pickles. Serve immediately.

Creamed Ham and Eggs

Ingredients

3 tablespoons butter or margarine
1/4 cup all-purpose flour
1/2 teaspoon dry mustard
1/8 teaspoon pepper
2 cups milk
1/2 teaspoon Worcestershire sauce
3 hard-cooked eggs, diced
2 cups cubed fully cooked ham
3 slices toast, cut into triangles

Directions

In a saucepan, melt butter. Add flour, mustard and pepper; cook until bubbly. Gradually add milk and Worcestershire sauce; cook and stir until thickened. Stir in eggs and ham, heat through. Serve hot over toast.

Veggie Poached Eggs

Ingredients

1 1/2 tablespoons olive oil
1 cup fresh asparagus, trimmed and coarsely chopped
1 cup carrots, julienned
1/4 cup spaghetti sauce
4 eggs
salt and pepper to taste

Directions

In a large frying pan, heat the oil over medium high heat. Add the asparagus, carrots and spaghetti sauce; cook on medium high heat until vegetables are soft. You may add a little water if necessary.

Push the vegetables to the side of the pan to create four spaces for the eggs. Crack eggs directly into the holes, being careful not to break the yolk. Cook until eggs are done, but the yolk is still soft. Season with salt and pepper to taste. Remove from heat and serve immediately.

Scrambled Eggs and Tomatoes

Ingredients

2 large eggs, beaten
2 tomatoes, coarsely chopped
1 1/2 teaspoons sugar
salt to taste
1 dash soy sauce

Directions

In a skillet over medium heat, scramble eggs until almost done. Remove to a plate.

Return skillet to medium heat, and stir in tomatoes. Cook 2 to 3 minutes. Stir in sugar, salt, and soy. Return eggs to skillet; cook, stirring, about 1 minute more.

Creamed Eggs

Ingredients

6 eggs
2 tablespoons butter
2 tablespoons all-purpose flour
2 cups milk
1/8 teaspoon ground white pepper, if desired
salt and pepper to taste

Directions

Place egg in a saucepan and cover with cold water. Bring water to a boil and immediately remove from heat. Cover and let eggs stand in hot water for 10 to 12 minutes. Remove from hot water, cool, peel and chop.

Melt butter in saucepan, add flour until it forms into a ball. Slowly add the milk and stir until the sauce comes to a boil.

Stir the white pepper, salt, black pepper, and chopped eggs into the sauce; stir until the eggs are heated.

Wrapped Mexican Eggs

Ingredients

1 1/2 pounds tomatillos, husked and cut in half
2 cloves garlic, halved
1 1/2 cups chopped onion
1/3 cup chopped fresh cilantro
1 cup water
1 jalapeno pepper, seeded and minced
1 1/2 teaspoons salt
4 tomatoes, chopped
1 tablespoon olive oil
2 green bell pepper, thinly sliced
16 eggs, beaten
1 teaspoon salt
ground black pepper to taste
1 1/2 cups shredded Monterey Jack cheese
8 (12 inch) flour tortillas
1/2 cup sour cream

Directions

Preheat oven to 375 degrees F (190 degrees C).

Make the salsa: In a blender or food processor puree tomatillos, garlic, onions, cilantro, water, jalapeno pepper and salt. In a saucepan, bring the salsa to a simmer. Simmer for 5 minutes. Transfer the salsa into a bowl and set the bowl aside.

Make the filling: Put the chopped tomatoes into a sieve, and let them drain for 10 minutes or more.

In a large skillet, heat the oil over medium heat. Add the bell peppers, and saute them until they are soft, about 5 to 10 minutes. Add the eggs, and turn the heat to low. Stirring occasionally with a wooden spoon, let the eggs cook until they begin to set. Take the skillet off the heat and sprinkle in the salt, pepper, 1 cup Monterey Jack cheese and the drained tomatoes; stir gently.

Lay a flour tortilla on a work surface. Spread about 2/3 cup of the egg filling down the middle of the tortilla. Drop 1 tablespoon of the sour cream on top of the eggs. Fold in the sides of the tortilla to partly cover the egg mixture, then roll the tortilla, folding in the outer edges as you roll, to enclose the egg mixture completely. Continue this process with the remaining filling and the tortillas.

Place the filled tortillas close together in a 10x16 inch casserole dish. At this point you can cover the dish and chill it for up to 24 hours.

Pour the salsa over the filled tortillas, and sprinkle them with the 1/2 cup grated cheese. Cover the dish with foil, and bake the casserole for 15 minutes (25 minutes if it has been chilled). Serve hot.

Greek Cowboy Hash and Eggs

Ingredients

2 tablespoons olive oil
1 large sweet potato, peeled and cut into 1/4-inch cubes
1 red onion, chopped
4 cloves garlic, minced
1 tablespoon chipotle chile powder
1 teaspoon ground cumin
1 teaspoon ground coriander
salt and ground black pepper to taste
2 tablespoons olive oil
4 eggs
1/4 cup fresh cilantro, chopped
1/2 cup crumbled feta cheese
1/2 avocado, sliced

Directions

Heat 2 tablespoons olive oil in a skillet over medium heat. Cook the potatoes in the heated oil until they begin to soften, about 5 minutes. Add the onion and garlic; continue cooking until the onions sweat and begin to caramelize. Season with chipotle chile powder, cumin, coriander, salt, and pepper; stir. Transfer to a bowl and cover with a plate to retain the heat.

Pour 2 tablespoons olive oil into the skillet and return to medium heat. Crack the eggs into the heated oil and cook until they begin to turn opaque; flip and continue cooking until no clear white remains. (DonвЂ™t overcook the eggs -- the best part of this meal is the smoothness that the yolk adds to the mix). Place the cooked eggs atop the potato mixture. Top with cilantro, feta cheese, and avocado to serve.

Scotch Eggs

Ingredients

1 pound pork sausage meat
2 teaspoons Worcestershire sauce
4 hard-cooked eggs, peeled
1 tablespoon all-purpose flour
1/8 teaspoon salt
1/8 teaspoon ground black pepper
1 egg, beaten
2/3 cup dry bread crumbs
1 quart oil for deep frying

Directions

In a medium bowl, mix together the pork sausage and Worcestershire sauce. Combine the flour, salt and pepper; mix into the sausage.

Divide the sausage into four equal parts. Mold each part around one of the hard-cooked eggs, rolling between your hands to shape.
Place the beaten egg and bread crumbs into separate dishes. Dip the balls into the egg, then roll in the bread crumbs until coated. Shake off any excess.

Heat the oil in a large saucepan or deep fryer to 365 degrees F (180 degrees C), or until a cube of bread dropped into the oil turns brown in 1 minute. Lower the eggs carefully into the hot oil. Fry for 5 minutes, or until deep golden brown.

Hearty Scrambled Eggs

Ingredients

8 eggs
1 1/4 cups diced fully cooked ham
3/4 cup diced Cheddar cheese
1/2 cup chopped fresh
mushrooms
1/4 cup chopped onion
2 tablespoons butter or margarine

Directions

In a bowl, beat eggs. Add ham, cheese, mushrooms and onion. Melt butter in a skillet; add egg mixture. Cook and stir over medium heat until eggs are completely set and cheese is melted.

Lightly Scrambled Eggs

Ingredients

9 egg whites
3 eggs
1/2 cup reduced-fat sour cream
1/4 cup fat-free milk
2 green onions, thinly sliced
1/4 teaspoon salt
1/8 teaspoon pepper
6 drops yellow food coloring
3/4 cup shredded reduced-fat
Cheddar cheese

Directions

In a large bowl, whisk the egg whites and eggs. Add the sour cream, milk, onions, salt, pepper and food coloring if desired. Pour into a large nonstick skillet coated with nonstick cooking spray; cook and gently stir over medium heat until eggs are completely set. Remove from the heat. Sprinkle with cheese; cover and let stand for 5 minutes to allow cheese to melt.

Eggs Avocado Benedict Style

Ingredients

1 Chilean Hass avocado
2 tablespoons lemon juice
1/2 teaspoon salt
Dash cayenne pepper
4 slices turkey or regular Canadian bacon
2 English muffins, split and toasted
4 eggs, poached
Parsley or other fresh herbs, for garnish

Directions

Rinse avocados, cut in half and remove the pit. Spoon avocado into a zip top plastic bag. Add lemon juice, salt and pepper. Press out air and seal bag. Cut off tip of one end of bag. In skillet, cook Canadian bacon until hot and lightly browned around edges. Place one slice of Canadian bacon on each muffin half. Top with poached egg. Pipe avocado spread over egg.

Scrambled Eggs Done Right

Ingredients

2 eggs
1 teaspoon mayonnaise or salad dressing
1 teaspoon water (optional)
1 teaspoon margarine or butter
salt and pepper to taste (optional)

Directions

In a cup or small bowl, whisk together the eggs, mayonnaise and water using a fork. Melt margarine in a skillet over low heat. Pour in the eggs, and stir constantly as they cook. Remove the eggs to a plate when they are set, but still moist. Do not over cook. Never add salt or pepper until eggs are on plate, but these are also good without.

Poached Eggs and Asparagus

Ingredients

4 eggs
1 cube chicken bouillon (optional)
1 pound fresh asparagus, trimmed
4 slices whole wheat bread
4 slices Cheddar cheese
1 tablespoon butter
salt and pepper to taste

Directions

Fill a saucepan half way full of water. Bring to a boil and stir in the bouillon cube until dissolved. Crack one egg into a measuring cup or large spoon and gently slip it into the boiling water. Repeat with remaining eggs. Simmer for about 5 minutes over medium heat. Remove with a slotted spoon and keep warm

Meanwhile, Place the asparagus into a saucepan and fill with enough water to cover. Bring to a boil, and cook until asparagus is tender, about 4 minutes. Drain.

Toast the bread to your desired darkness. Spread butter onto each piece of toast. Top with a slice of cheese, then a poached egg and finally, asparagus. Season with salt and pepper and serve immediately.

Buffet Scrambled Eggs

Ingredients

4 tablespoons butter or margarine, divided
2 tablespoons all-purpose flour
1 cup milk
2 teaspoons chicken bouillon granules
8 eggs, beaten
Minced fresh parsley

Directions

In a saucepan, melt 2 tablespoons butter. Stir in flour until smooth. Add milk and bouillon. Bring to a boil; cook and stir for 2 minutes or until thickened. Set aside.

In a large skillet, melt remaining butter. Add eggs; cook over medium heat until eggs begin to set, stirring occasionally. Add white sauce; mix well. Cook until the eggs are completely set. Garnish with parsley if desired.

Pickled Eggs II

Ingredients

12 extra large eggs
1 1/2 cups distilled white vinegar
1 1/2 cups water
1 tablespoon pickling spice
1 clove garlic, crushed
1 bay leaf

Directions

Place eggs in a medium saucepan and cover with cold water. Bring water to a boil and immediately remove from heat. Cover and let eggs stand in hot water for 10 to 12 minutes. Remove from hot water, cool and peel.

In a medium saucepan over medium heat, mix together the vinegar, water and pickling spice. Bring to a boil and mix in the garlic and bay leaf. Remove from heat.

Transfer the eggs to sterile containers. Fill the containers with the hot vinegar mixture, seal and refrigerate 8 to 10 days before serving.

Eggs with Tomatoes

Ingredients

2 tablespoons sunflower seed oil
4 large tomatoes, sliced
1 (6 ounce) can tomato paste
1 teaspoon ground cumin
1 teaspoon ground allspice
1 teaspoon salt
4 eggs, beaten

Directions

Heat the sunflower seed oil in a large skillet over medium heat. Stir in the tomatoes, and evenly coat in the oil. Mix in the tomato paste, and season with cumin, allspice, and salt. Cover, and cook until the tomatoes are tender, about 10 minutes.

Pour the eggs over the tomato mixture. Cover, and continue cooking 10 minutes, or until the eggs are no longer runny.

Deviled Eggs II

Ingredients

6 eggs
1 teaspoon white vinegar
1 tablespoon mayonnaise 1/4
teaspoon prepared mustard salt
and pepper to taste
1 teaspoon paprika
2 leaves of lettuce

Directions

Place eggs in a pot of salted water. Bring the water to a boil, and let eggs cook in boiling water until they are hard boiled, approximately 10 to 15 minutes. Drain eggs, and let cool. Once cool, remove the shell, cut the eggs in half lengthwise and scoop out the yolks.

Place the yolks in a medium-size mixing bowl and mash them. Blend in vinegar, mayonnaise, mustard, salt and pepper. You may need to add more mayonnaise to hold the mixture together, but it should be slightly dry.

Carefully put the egg yolk mixture back into the egg whites but do not pack it. There will be enough mixture so the whites are overfilled. Sprinkle with paprika. Place on bed of lettuce and/or garnish with parsley. Cool before serving.

Greek Scrambled Eggs

Ingredients

1 tablespoon butter
3 eggs
1 teaspoon water
1/2 cup crumbled feta cheese
salt and pepper to taste

Directions

Heat butter in a skillet over medium-high heat. Beat eggs and water together, then pour into pan. Add feta cheese, and cook, stirring occasionally to scramble. Season with salt and pepper.

Cheesy Herbed Eggs

Ingredients

1 1/3 cups light cream
1 teaspoon grated lemon peel
16 eggs, lightly beaten
1 teaspoon salt
1/2 teaspoon white pepper
1/4 teaspoon dried basil
1/4 teaspoon dried oregano
1/4 teaspoon crushed dried rosemary
1/2 cup shredded Cheddar cheese
1/2 cup grated Parmesan cheese
1/4 cup butter or margarine
Tomato Wedges

Directions

In a large bowl, combine cream and lemon peel. Add eggs and seasonings; mix well. Stir in cheeses. In a large skillet, melt butter; pour in egg mixture. Cook and stir gently over medium heat until eggs are set, about 15 minutes. Garnish with tomato wedges if desired.

Divine Hard-Boiled Eggs

Ingredients

12 eggs

Directions

Place eggs in a pot; pour enough water over the eggs to cover. Cover and turn stove to high; bring to a boil; turn off heat and place pot on a cool burner. Let the pot sit with the cover on for 15 minutes. Meanwhile, fill a large bowl halfway with cold water; transfer the eggs from the pot to the cold water. Replace the water with cold water as needed to keep cold until the eggs are completely cooled. Chill in refrigerator at least 2 hours before peeling.

Potato Salad Deviled Eggs

Ingredients

8 eggs
1 large potato, coarsely chopped
2 teaspoons pickle relish
2 teaspoons mustard
4 teaspoons creamy salad dressing (such as Miracle Whip®)
salt to taste
ground black pepper to taste
paprika for garnish

Directions

Place the eggs into a saucepan in a single layer and fill with water to cover the eggs by 1 inch. Cover the saucepan and bring the water to a boil over high heat. Once the water is boiling, remove from the heat and let the eggs stand in the hot water for 15 minutes. Pour out the hot water, then cool the eggs under cold running water in the sink. Peel once cold. Slice the cooled eggs in half lengthwise, and scoop out and reserve the yolks.

While the eggs are cooking, place the cut-up potato into a saucepan with water to cover, bring to a boil, reduce heat, and simmer until the potato pieces are tender, 10 to 15 minutes. Drain the potato, and let cool.

In a bowl, mash the reserved egg yolks with pickle relish, mustard, creamy dressing, salt, and pepper until well combined. Place the potato into a bowl, and coarsely mash with a fork. Lightly combine the potato with the yolk mixture. Stuff each egg half generously with potato salad, and sprinkle with paprika. Cover and chill until ready to serve, at least 20 minutes.

Easy Armadillo Eggs

Ingredients

1 (8 ounce) package cream cheese, softened
1/4 cup bacon bits
1 tablespoon chopped fresh chives
1 teaspoon hot sauce
1 pound pork sausage
1 cup shredded Cheddar cheese
1 (5.5 ounce) package seasoned coating mix
1/8 teaspoon ground cumin
1/8 teaspoon chili powder
16 fresh jalapeno peppers

Directions

Preheat oven to 350 degrees F (175 degrees C).

In a bowl, mix the cream cheese, bacon bits, chives, and hot sauce. In a separate bowl, mix the uncooked sausage and Cheddar cheese. On a flat surface, mix the seasoned coating mix, cumin, and chili powder.

Cut a slit lengthwise into each jalapeno pepper, and remove the seeds. Stuff the peppers with the cream cheese mixture. Press the sausage mixture around the stuffed jalapenos, and roll in the seasoned coating mix to coat.

Arrange the coated jalapenos on a baking sheet in a single layer. Bake 25 minutes in the preheated oven, until the sausage is evenly brown.

Telur Balado (Spicy Chile Sauce with Eggs)

Ingredients

1 cup vegetable oil for frying
6 hard-boiled eggs, shells removed
6 red chile peppers, seeded and chopped
4 cloves garlic
4 medium shallots
2 tomatoes, quartered
1 teaspoon shrimp paste
1 1/2 tablespoons peanut oil
1 tablespoon vegetable oil
1 teaspoon white vinegar
1 teaspoon white sugar
salt and pepper to taste

Directions

Heat 1 cup oil in a small saucepan over medium-high heat. Deep fry the eggs in the hot oil until they are golden brown, 5 to 7 minutes; set aside.

Combine the chile peppers, garlic, shallots, tomatoes, and shrimp paste in a food processor; blend into a paste. Add in peanut oil. Process again until smooth.

Heat 1 tablespoon oil in a large skillet over medium heat. Pour the chile pepper mixture into the skillet. Stir the vinegar, sugar, salt, and pepper into the mixture. Add the fried eggs to the mixture, turning to coat. Reduce heat to medium-low; simmer until fragrant, about 5 minutes.

Ham and Mushroom Baked Eggs

Ingredients

3 tablespoons butter
3 tablespoons all-purpose flour
2 cups milk
1/2 teaspoon salt
1/8 teaspoon ground black pepper
1 cup shredded sharp Cheddar cheese
3 tablespoons butter
1/4 cup diced onion
12 eggs, beaten
1 cup diced ham
6 small mushrooms, chopped

Directions

Make the cheese sauce: Melt 3 tablespoons butter in a saucepan on top of the stove. Quickly stir the flour into the saucepan until the mixture is smooth. Stir in the milk, salt and pepper; continue stirring until the mixture is smooth and thick. Finally, stir in the cheese until it is melted.

Grease a 9x13 inch baking pan.

In a skillet, saute butter and onions. Pour the beaten eggs and ham into the skillet; scramble until set. Fold the mushrooms and cheese sauce into the eggs. Pour the mixture into the prepared baking pan. Cover and chill for 30 minutes or overnight.

Preheat oven to 350 degrees F (175 degrees C).

Bake the egg and mushroom casserole for 30 minutes in the 350 degrees F (175 degrees C) oven.

Mustard Pickled Eggs

Ingredients

6 hard-cooked eggs
1/2 teaspoon mustard powder
1 1/2 teaspoons cornstarch
1 teaspoon white sugar
1/2 teaspoon ground turmeric
1 teaspoon salt
2 cups apple cider vinegar

Directions

Place the hard-cooked eggs into a 1 quart jar. In a saucepan, stir together the mustard, cornstarch, sugar, turmeric, and salt. Pour in just enough of the cider vinegar to make a paste, then gradually stir in the rest. Bring the mixture to a boil, stirring frequently. Pour into the jars with the eggs. Put the lid on the jar, and refrigerate for a few days before eating for best flavor.

Oriental Tea Leaf Eggs

Ingredients

1 tablespoon black tea leaves
2 (3 inch) cinnamon sticks
4 whole star anise pods
1 tablespoon five-spice powder
6 whole cloves
1 slice fresh ginger root
1/2 teaspoon Szechuan peppercorns
1 teaspoon licorice root
1 piece dried mandarin orange peel
1 ounce Chinese rock sugar
1/2 cup dark soy sauce
1/3 cup light-colored soy sauce
10 hard-cooked eggs

Directions

Place the tea, cinnamon, star anise, five-spice, cloves, ginger, peppercorns, licorice, orange peel, rock sugar, dark soy sauce, and light soy sauce in a large saucepan. Bring to a boil, then reduce heat to medium-low, and let simmer for 15 minutes. Meanwhile, lightly tap the hard-cooked eggs to crack the shells all over. The soy sauce will penetrate the cracks, and color the egg white.

Place the eggs in the simmering liquid, and cook for 30 minutes, then remove from the heat, and let the eggs stand in the liquid for 2 hours off the heat. After 2 hours, drain the eggs, chill, and peel.

BBQ Eggs

Ingredients

4 eggs
2 1/2 tablespoons barbecue sauce
2 tablespoons milk
1 1/2 teaspoons dried dill
1 1/2 teaspoons mustard powder
1 1/2 teaspoons minced garlic
1 tablespoon butter or margarine
1/2 cup shredded Cheddar cheese

Directions

In a medium bowl, whisk together the eggs, barbeque sauce, milk, dill, mustard powder and garlic.

Melt butter or margarine in a large skillet over medium heat. Pour in the egg mixture, and cook stirring frequently until eggs are scrambled and cooked through. Remove from heat, and sprinkle cheese over the top. Let stand for a minute to melt cheese, then serve immediately.

Polished Eggs

Ingredients

2 tablespoons vegetable oil
4 cloves crushed garlic
2 tablespoons brown sugar
4 tablespoons soy sauce
4 eggs

Directions

Place eggs in a saucepan, and cover completely with cold water. Bring water to a boil for one minute. Cover, remove from heat, and let eggs stand in hot water for 10 to 12 minutes. Remove from hot water, and cool. Peel. Score spirals into the white of the eggs, from the tops to the bottoms, using a sharp knife.

In a small saucepan, heat oil. Add garlic, and cook over medium heat until it begins to brown. Stir in sugar and soy sauce. Remove pan from heat.

Place eggs in sauce, and turn to coat. When eggs are nice and dark, and the sauce is thick and syrupy, remove from sauce. Serve.

Pickled Red Beet Eggs

Ingredients

1 (15 ounce) can beets
1 onion, thinly sliced
12 hard cooked eggs, shelled and left whole
1/4 cup white sugar
1/2 cup vinegar

Directions

Drain liquid from the beets into saucepan. Place beets, onions, and eggs into a large bowl or pitcher.

Pour sugar and vinegar into the saucepan with the beet liquid and bring the mixture to a boil. Reduce the heat to low, and let the mixture simmer 15 minutes.

Pour the beet juice mixture over the beets, eggs, and onions. Seal the bowl or pitcher and refrigerate. Refrigerate for at least one to 3 days; the longer they are allowed to sit the better they will taste.

Eggs Royale

Ingredients

2 1/2 cups seasoned croutons
1 1/2 cups shredded Cheddar cheese
4 eggs
2 cups milk
1/2 teaspoon dry mustard
1/2 teaspoon salt
1/4 teaspoon onion powder
1/8 teaspoon pepper
10 bacon strips, cooked and crumbled

Directions

Place croutons in a greased 13-in. x 9-in. x 2-in. baking dish. Cover with cheese. In a bowl, beat eggs, milk, mustard, salt onion powder and pepper; pour over cheese. Sprinkle with bacon. Cover and chill 8 hours or overnight. Remove from refrigerator 30 minutes before baking. Bake, uncovered, at 350 degrees F for 30-40 minutes, or until a knife inserted near the center comes out clean. Let stand 5 minutes before cutting.

Vegetable Scrambled Eggs

Ingredients

4 eggs
1/2 cup chopped green pepper
1/4 cup milk
1/4 cup sliced green onions
1/2 teaspoon salt
1/8 teaspoon pepper
1 small tomato, seeded and chopped

Directions

In a small bowl, beat eggs. Add green pepper, milk, onions, salt and pepper. Pour into a lightly greased skillet. Cook and stir over medium heat until eggs are nearly set. Add the tomato; cook and stir until heated through.

Pickled Eggs

Ingredients

1 (15 ounce) can red beets
1/4 cup brown sugar
1/2 cup white vinegar
1/2 cup cold water 1/2
teaspoon salt
4 whole cloves
1 small cinnamon stick
6 hard-cooked eggs

Directions

Pour the beet juice into a medium-size pot. Stir in the brown sugar, vinegar, water, salt, cloves, and the cinnamon stick. Place the pot over a medium heat for 8 minutes, stirring occasionally.

Place the beets into the liquid mixture and let it cook for an additional 2 minutes to allow the beets to heat.

Place the hard cooked eggs (with the shells removed) in a container with a tight-fitting lid. Pour the liquid and beets into the container with the eggs. Store the container in the refrigerator for approximately 5 days before eating.

Rita's Eggs Strata

Ingredients

10 slices stale white bread
1/4 cup butter, softened
3 cups shredded Cheddar cheese
3 cups shredded Monterey Jack cheese
8 eggs, beaten
2 cups half-and-half cream
2 cups milk
1 teaspoon brown sugar
1/4 teaspoon paprika
1 1/2 teaspoons salt
1/2 teaspoon ground black pepper
1/8 teaspoon cayenne pepper
1/2 teaspoon onion powder
1 teaspoon mustard powder
1 teaspoon Worcestershire sauce
1 tablespoon chopped fresh parsley for garnish

Directions

Spread butter onto one side of each slice of bread. Cut into quarters. Lay half of the bread, butter side down, in the bottom of a 9x13 inch baking dish. Top with half of the Cheddar cheese and half of the Monterey Jack. Layer the remaining bread over the cheese, and top with the other halves of the cheeses.

In a large bowl, whisk together the eggs, half-and-half, and milk. Stir in the brown sugar, salt, pepper, cayenne, onion powder, mustard powder, and Worcestershire sauce. Pour over the cheese and bread. Cover, and refrigerate at least 6 hours, preferably overnight.

Preheat the oven to 325 degrees F (165 degrees C). Bake the strata uncovered for 1 hour in the preheated oven. Let stand for 10 minutes before serving. Slice and garnish with fresh parsley.

Armadillo Eggs

Ingredients

24 jalapeno peppers
1 pound sausage
2 cups all-purpose baking mix
1 (16 ounce) package Cheddar cheese, shredded
1 tablespoon crushed red pepper flakes
1 tablespoon garlic salt
1 (16 ounce) package Monterey Jack cheese, cubed

Directions

Preheat oven to 325 degrees F (165 degrees C). Lightly grease a medium baking sheet.

Cut a slit in each jalapeno pepper. Remove and discard seeds and pulp.

In a medium bowl, mix sausage, baking mix, Cheddar cheese, crushed red pepper, and garlic salt.

Stuff jalapenos with the Monterey Jack cheese cubes. Shape sausage mixture around the jalapenos to form balls.

Arrange jalapeno balls on the prepared baking sheet. Bake 25 minutes in the preheated oven, until lightly browned.

Eggs and Spaghetti

Ingredients

4 ounces spaghetti
2 tablespoons butter
2 eggs
2 teaspoons garlic powder
2 teaspoons ground black pepper
1 tablespoon minced onion
1 tablespoon dried rosemary

Directions

Bring a large pot of lightly salted water to a boil. Add pasta and cook for 8 to 10 minutes or until al dente; drain.

Meanwhile, in a large skillet melt butter over medium heat; cook eggs sunny-side up (so that egg yolks are not broken). Sprinkle garlic powder, ground black pepper, onion and rosemary on eggs while cooking.

Place hot pasta and cooked eggs on a plate and stir together; the broken yolks will create the sauce. Serve hot.

Deviled Eggs with Zip

Ingredients

12 eggs
2 tablespoons mayonnaise
1 teaspoon Chinese hot prepared mustard
2 teaspoons yellow mustard
salt and pepper to taste
paprika, for garnish

Directions

Place eggs in a large saucepan and cover with cold water. Bring water to a boil and immediately remove from heat. Cover and let eggs stand in hot water for 10 to 12 minutes. Remove from hot water, cool and peel.

Slice eggs in half lengthwise and remove yolks. Place yolks in a medium bowl, and mash together with mayonnaise, Chinese hot prepared mustard, yellow mustard, salt and pepper.

Fill the hollowed egg whites with the egg yolk mixture. Garnish with paprika. Chill in the refrigerator until serving.

Mother-In-Law Eggs

Ingredients

6 eggs
2 tablespoons mayonnaise
1 tablespoon spicy brown
mustard (such as Gulden's®)
1 teaspoon hot mustard (such as
Sweet Hot Mister Mustard®)
1 teaspoon white sugar
salt and pepper to taste
paprika for garnish (optional)
6 pimento-stuffed green olives,
cut in half

Directions

Place the eggs into a saucepan in a single layer and fill with water to cover the eggs by 1 inch. Cover the saucepan and bring the water to a boil over high heat. Remove from the heat and let the eggs stand in the hot water for 15 minutes. Drain. Cool the eggs under cold running water. Peel once cold. Halve the eggs lengthwise and scoop the yolks into a bowl. Mash the yolks with a fork.

Stir the mayonnaise, spicy brown mustard, hot mustard, sugar, salt, and pepper into the yolks until well combined. Spoon into a quart-size, resealable plastic bag. Snip a corner off the plastic bag.

Squeeze the yolk mixture into the egg halves, sprinkle each stuffed egg with paprika, and top with an olive half.

Three-Cheese Deviled Eggs

Ingredients

6 hard-cooked eggs
3/4 cup mayonnaise
2 tablespoons finely shredded Monterey Jack cheese
2 tablespoons finely shredded Swiss cheese
2 tablespoons minced chives, divided
1/8 teaspoon ground mustard
1/8 teaspoon pepper
2 ounces processed cheese food (eg. Velveeta), cubed
1 dash paprika

Directions

Cut eggs in half lengthwise. Remove yolks; set whites aside. In a bowl, mash the yolks. Add the mayonnaise, shredded cheeses, 1 tablespoon chives, mustard and pepper. In a microwave-safe bowl, melt the process cheese on high for 1-2 minutes; stir until smooth. Stir into yolk mixture. Pipe or spoon into egg whites. Sprinkle with paprika and remaining chives. Refrigerate until serving.